About Reptiles

About Reptiles

A Guide for Children

Cathryn Sill

Illustrated by John Sill

McGraw Hill SRA

Columbus, OH

For the One who created reptiles.

—*Genesis* 1:24

First published in the United States under the title ABOUT REPTILES: A GUIDE FOR CHILDREN by Cathryn Sill, illustrated By John C. Sill. Text Copyright © 1997, 1999 by Cathryn P. Sill. Illustrations Copyright (c) 1991, 1997, 2013 by John C. Sill. Published by arrangement with Peachtree Publishers.

SRAonline.com

McGraw Hill SRA

Printed in the United States of America.

Send all inquiries to:
SRA/McGraw-Hill
4400 Easton Commons
Columbus, OH 43219-6188

ISBN 978-0-07-612516-6
MHID 0-07-612516-5

8 9 10 11 12 LHN 20 19 18 17

The McGraw-Hill Companies

About Reptiles

Reptiles have dry, scaly skin.

PLATE 1
Rough Green Snake

Some reptiles have a hard, bony plate.

PLATE 2
Eastern Box Turtle

Reptiles have short legs …

PLATE 3
Texas Horned Lizard

or no legs at all.

PLATE 4
Slender Glass Lizard

They move by crawling …

PLATE 5
Five-lined Skink

or by swimming.

PLATE 6
Green Turtle

Reptiles need warm temperatures.

PLATE 7
Collared Lizard

They hibernate in cold, winter weather.

PLATE 8
Painted Turtle

Most reptiles are meat eaters.

PLATE 9
Corn Snake

A few eat meat and plants.

PLATE 10
Desert Tortoise

Some reptiles use venom to capture their prey.

PLATE 11
Eastern Diamondback Rattlesnake

Baby reptiles hatch from eggs.

PLATE 12
American Alligators

In some reptiles, the mother carries the eggs inside her body until they are ready to hatch.

PLATE 13
Common Garter Snake

Young reptiles care for themselves as soon as they hatch.

PLATE 14
Loggerhead Turtles

Reptiles are important to us.

PLATE 15
Green Anole

Afterword

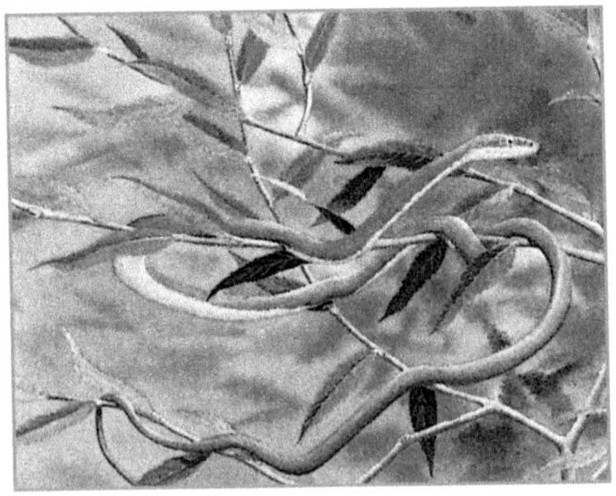

PLATE 1
The scales of reptiles are formed by folds in the skin. The skin has few pores, so it is dry. All reptiles shed their skin. Lizards shed theirs bit by bit, but snakes shed their entire skin in one long piece. Rough green snakes are tree dwellers that eat insects, caterpillars, and spiders.

PLATE 2
The protective shells of turtles are their most characteristic feature. Eastern box turtles live in moist forests, meadows, and floodplains. Box turtles have been known to live over a hundred years. They eat berries, mushrooms, slugs, and earthworms.

PLATE 3
Texas horned lizards are commonly called "horned toads." Their spines serve as protection, and their bodies will inflate with air to make it hard for another animal to swallow them. If these forms of defense fail, Texas horned lizards can squirt a stream of blood from the corners of their eyes to repel predators.

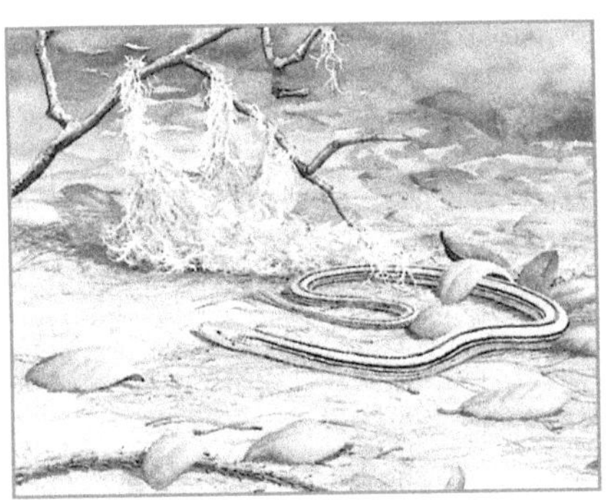

PLATE 4
Slender glass lizards are legless lizards. They get their name from their tail which, when grabbed, will shatter into several pieces. Slender glass lizards live in dry grassland and dry, open woods.

PLATE 5
Five-lined skinks live on damp ground in woodlands. They may be seen in gardens and around houses. Young five-lined skinks have a bright blue tail that changes to brown as they mature.

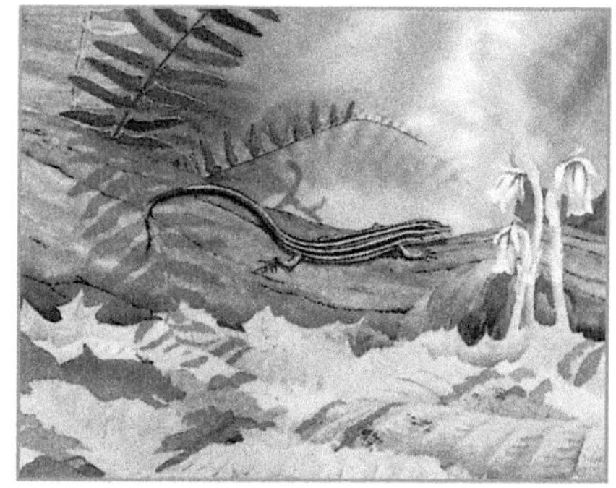

PLATE 6
Green turtles live in warm waters of both the Atlantic and Pacific Oceans. Green turtle numbers have been declining rapidly because their meat, flipper leather, and oil are used by peoples all over the world.

PLATE 7
Unlike mammals and birds, which are both warm-blooded, reptiles' bodies are the same temperature as their surroundings. Collared lizards are aggressive and eat insects, other lizards, and even small snakes. When fleeing predators, they run on their hind legs, looking like tiny dinosaurs.

PLATE 8
Painted turtles are probably the most common small-pond turtle in North America. They live in shallow water and are often seen basking in the sun on logs. When painted turtles hibernate, they bury themselves in mud under water.

PLATE 9
Corn snakes probably get their name from their checkered belly scales, which look like the kernels of Indian corn. They are good climbers, but they are more likely to be found on the ground of underground in rodent burrows.

PLATE 10
Desert tortoises feed during the morning and late afternoon. They dig burrows, where they retreat during the heat of the day. Desert tortoises are an endangered species and are protected from being gathered for the pet market.

PLATE 11
Eastern diamondback rattlesnakes are the largest and most venomous snakes in North America. The record length for an eastern diamondback is eight feet. They eat rabbits, rodents, and birds.

PLATE 12
American alligators are the largest reptile in North America. Adults generally range six to twelve feet in length. Female alligators build nests by mounding mud and vegetation, using their lower jaws as a scoop. They lay twenty to seventy eggs in the nest and guard it for two and one-half months until the young hatch.

PLATE 13

Common garter snakes are the most widely distributed snake in North America. They are found in a variety of habitats, including meadows, marshes, woodlands, along streams and drainage ditches, and in farms, city lots, and parks.

PLATE 14

Loggerhead turtles are the most common sea turtle in the waters off of North America. They have been reported to grow up to seven feet long and weigh up to one thousand pounds. Many nesting sites of the loggerhead have been destroyed by beach development.

PLATE 15

Green anoles are abundant in the American South. They are found on fences, around old buildings, on shrubs, and in trees. Reptiles provide the valuable service of eating many harmful rodents and insects.

Cathryn Sill, a former elemetary school teacher, is the author of the acclaimed ABOUT... series. With her husband John and her brother-in-law Ben Sill, she coauthored the popular bird-guide parodies, A FIELD GUIDE TO LITTLE-KNOWN AND SELDOM-SEEN BIRDS OF NORTH AMERICA, ANOTHER FIELD GUIDE TO LITTLE-KNOWN AND SELDOM-SEEN BIRDS OF NORTH AMERICA, and BEYOND BIRDWATCHING, all from Peachtree Publishers.

John Sill is a prize-winning and widely published wildlife artist who illustrated the ABOUT... series and coauthored the FIELD GUIDES and BEYOND BIRDWATCHING. A native of North Carolina, he holds a B.S. in Wildlife Biology from North Carolina State University.

The Sills live and work in Franklin, North Carolina.